the **passage** of **bees**

Also by Michele Fermanis-Winward
and published by Ginninderra Press
Threading Raindrops
The Eucalypt Distillery
A Larrikin in the Blood
These Weighted Months
The Symbiotic Web
Aquamarine
To the Dam (Pocket Poets)
The Sail Weaver (Pocket Poets)
Curdled Milk (Pocket Poets)

the
passage
of bees

Michele Fermanis-Winward

The Passage of Bees
ISBN Paperback: 9781761099069
ISBN Ebook: 9781761099076
Copyright © text Michele Fermanis-Winward 2025

Cover image: Michele Fermanis-Winward

with thanks to Molly's bees.

First published 2025 by
GINNINDERRA PRESS
PO Box 2 Bentleigh 3204
ginninderrapress.com.au

Contents

Introduction	9
Opening	11
Buzzed	12
One September Morning	13
Radiant	14
The Laburnum Party	15
This Futile, Thankful Task	16
Immortality	17
Sunshine Angels	18
The Dancers	19
The Gift	20
Enter the Sun	21
In Essence	22
The Greeting	23
The Rambler	24
Moments of Grace	25
Cabbage Whites	26
Dendrophilia	27
Green With Envy	28
Camellia Sasanqua	29
Persimmon	30
Symbiosis	31
The Passage of Bees	32
On Transience	34
Autumn April 25	35
Towards Winter	36
Waiting for the Wolf	37

After the Party	38
Gentle as a Falling Cloud	39
Nested	40
A Promise in Winter	41
Unwelcome	42
Aqua Vite	43
Cloudy With the Chance of Disaster	44
Enduring	45
I Listen to Their Passing	46
A Pledge	47
Mellifluous	48
No Second Coming, No Second Chance	49
Growth Overload	50
Splooshed	51
Still Life With Scrubbing Brush	52
Seeking Shelter	53
Lismore 2022	54
In the Shadow of Pompeii	55
Crystals and Carbon	56
Ghostly	57
In the Age of Extinctions	58
Finding Our Backbone	59
The Ancestors	60
On the Baaka	61
Seeds of War	62
With Wings to Fly	63
On Seeing	64
Marvels	65
From Where You Stand	66
This Sacred Life	67

Shanghaied	68
Those Indian Mynas	69
Exhaling	70
Dancing with Van Gogh	71
Free to Indulge	72
The Little Princess	73
Sandling	74
Unclocked	75
Weekending	76
The White-faced Heron	77
Time and Tide	78
Finding My Place	79
Acknowledgements	80

*Dedicated to the lives of bees,
who provide us with so much goodness.*

'That which is not good for the hive, is not good for the bee.'
— Marcus Aurelius

Introduction

This collection is a meditation on the garden that is my woodland sanctuary at the top of the Blue Mountains of New South Wales. Perched on the side of a ridge, it is sheltered by tall silver-top eucalypts with their rough grey bark. Each year, the number of insects, birds, reptiles and other animals declines, prey to loss of habitat and hard seasons.

In the south. the place of my birth, Melbourne's St Kilda by the bay holds inspiration of another kind. Here, I beachcomb, explore inner city lanes and markets, observe how we rub and fret against each other, the sharing, care and conflict that is part of community. The life unseen, of rodents and foxes, the introduced and native species continues around me.

Port Macquarie is my soul country, the ocean beaches, where for a few weeks each year I wander rocky headlands and spot dolphins and whales, watch pelicans, herons and brush turkeys.

These three places are my heartlands.

Opening

It starts, the change from grey and winter brown
you glance, as if from the corner of your eye
the palest nub of light on rough worn bark
next day it rains, returns to dull sky once again
you wait another week, trudge bare-branched paths
go out at last to bathe in sunshine on your skin
feel warmth seeping to your lungs and bones
note pale bronze, like soft fur upon a branch

each morning grows the covering of leaf
red-tinged or russet-edged, then opening
in multiples of shade, lime to veridian
ten, twenty, hundred fold, enough to please
the brush of a Van Gogh or Cézanne
an expanding palette, sun tempering each hue
until the scene is filled with green on green
rustling, thrusting, ever outward into life.

Buzzed

The bees are drunk on poppy pollen
doze in a nest of petals
luxuriate on crimson pillows
they forget themselves

their tasks abandoned
they dream of flower forests
while transparent wings
lift gently as they breathe

slowly they will rise
wobble to a laden neighbour
slide among its anthers
today the hive can wait.

One September Morning
i.m. Mary Oliver

I wake
and the rushing of the wind
to wherever it was going
has ceased
my small, warm dog
curled beside me, snores
there is no sound
beside hers and my own
grateful heart, softly purring
as a newborn day
opens into greeting
listen, you can hear it
singing in the trees.

Radiant

White blossom towers
above the house
bees dance in ecstasy
clouds puff, expose
dark underskirts
scent curls from hyacinths
that hug the ground

those crested bandits
bold cockatoos rule the yard
pluck tulip flowers
stems snap, leave petals
scattered in their wake
where once they also shone
luminous in white light.

The Laburnum Party

The setting is perfect
now everything is opening again
the crowd, food and drink
come together this warm day

as the flock is gathered
admiring all they find
laid out just for them
a high wind crashes in

uninvited, spoiling for action
he rattles heavy-laden branches
lashing out in all directions
sets golden cascades quaking

he whiplashes leggy boughs
bruises rise on petal skin
casting pollen in the air
nectar blown like urgent calls

guests mid food and drink
sent flying to dense forest
till the intruder is expelled
or finds another feast to plunder.

This Futile, Thankful Task

In the garden each day
my hands bend to the soil
this ancient ritual
creating order from abandon
taking and giving life

my homage through toil
in praise of the earth
soon the rain and sun
will cover these paths
in abundant heady growth

then snails and snakes
those silent watchful ones
can move unhindered
without my notice
taking and giving life.

Immortality

Just a clutch of leaves
reaching for the light
the stem grows hard
bending to its weight
upwards still it moves

above the height of man
buds forming at the tips
open to the night
the sun's hot force
causing it to wilt

the will to grow
then blossom into seed
this triumph of the flower
to attract a bee or moth
brings it everlasting life.

Sunshine Angels

We open like spring blossom
with the coming of the sun
too long the months of rain
grey skies would cloud our hearts

in the dawning light of summer
before the toll of heat
we celebrate our being
surrounded by new growth

there's a lustre on park trees
from stem to topmost leaf
the season when our lungs
breathe deep and spread like wings.

The Dancers

The curtain lifts   reveals
clear blue sky in spring's spotlight
birds pipe and flute
above the drum of trees

leaves bending to the wind
pirouette, en pointe
shake off their dusty coats
held close through winter months

the russet of emerging growth
on sun reflecting evergreens
the bend and flex of new stems
turbulence ripples through the air

responding to this power surge
a rise in sound   one thunderclap
blossoms swirling free, cascade
then cease as limbs relax and bow.

The Gift

The sound of rain
as it taps each leaf and stem
steady beating on the roof
flushing down the drain
its drum on stone and dirt

earth's song and timpani
the birds are silent, listening
to fat worms and grubs
moving through the soil
to beetles taking cover

as mice return to nests
until the storm has passed
petals fall, stems droop
the land and every living
thirsting mouth refreshed.

Enter the Sun

A currawong lilting through blue haze
writes its song upon my day
and I can hear a spinebill
as she whirs from flower to flower

these fragile, short lifespans
going through their ordinary ways
are balm to a mind that's clenched
I uncoil in their embrace.

In Essence

Tonight the air smells green
a tang of new mown grass
framed by the evening light

fresh particles of juice
lifted on a cooling breeze
and wafted into rooms

they provide a welcome draft
after days of sweated heat
their life distilled as scent.

The Greeting
for Stephen

One sliver of dawn light
slips through my curtain's edge
as a magpie unfurls its flag of notes
a distant truck grumbles towards the city

my small ball of dog gurgles in her sleep
while a wattlebird rackets a hole
within the waking sky, each in their way
celebrates another morning

the tolls of loss and need will come
add their weight onto the day
for now a spinebill trills, this fleeting gift
where all is well on earth.

The Rambler

Tight buds like any rose
that with the warmth unfurl

her untidy skirt of petals
and blousy open face

she is full blown too soon
no scent to draw us in

not your classic beauty
she is homely and unsung

in days full of sunshine
she lolls on drooping stems

growing ever outwards
to a sociable expanse

large hips of autumn's waning
spreading where she wants.

Moments of Grace

It is the solo currawong
chanting into distance
autumn mornings misted rain
the gathering of violet shadows

this summer's transit ends
as leaves form hands of flame
then crunch beneath my feet
in the bite of morning frost

it is a rug about me as I read
the music held in words
from the smallness of my life
to the depth of hearts and souls.

Cabbage Whites

The streets are filled with butterflies
dodging cars, rising
like weightless petals in spring sunshine
lilting over garden beds
chasing their last hours of life

they mate, lay one egg on a leaf, repeat
their offspring plump and velvety
feed on our juicy greens
just three weeks of life, but
they are the symbol of renewal and rebirth.

Dendrophilia

A lifelong love of trees
in all their wild precocity
diverse forms and texture
leaf shape and clinging bark
hold patterns for enchantment

dense canopy and sparse
their reassuring grace
of regrowth after storm
the will to live again
are lessons for the heart

my freedom to create
an oasis or a wooded glen
now twenty years on
my shaded paths and nooks
are deeply overgrown

brambles billow
snag unprotected skin
birds weave their songs
fledglings crash but never fall
through branches closely bound

a nest for weak and strong.

Green With Envy

They long to soar
and watch each bird
as it arrow darts or lopes
through clear and boundless air

from nub of sprout
this root bound horde
observe the feathered throng
who perch on branch and stem

they launch to flight
while trembling leaves remain
for they can't fly but curl and fall
to the waiting earth below.

Camellia Sasanqua

Limpid in soft morning light
their petals edged in pink
like hand-painted tissue paper

this flower of autumn's waning
whose cluster of yellow stamens
illuminates each heart

as a bee drawn to nectar
I step closer and inhale
the powdery almond scent

in the shortening of days
it fills my waking vision
is gone before I've drunk my fill.

Persimmon

for Rosalind

Through dense green canopy
the russet edged appear
some few at first
then vibrant orange spreads
each leaf is cleansed
by daily soaking rain

enclosed in fire
of red to yellow range
soft billows on the wind
this change outside my windowsill
the light it brings to sombre days
till one by one they fall

cast their embers to the ground
a warmth exchanged
for winter storms
bare branches swinging free
and I wrapped cosy still
in the memory of their flames.

Symbiosis

The wind rises
swirling rosy maple leaves
they tumble past wet branches
as the morning mist retreats

camellia petals fall
while honeyeaters pluck
their nectar-scented hearts
they too will feed soil life

the tree and bird in seasons
of growth into decline
the generosity of living
bound together on the earth.

The Passage of Bees

This whole day
its finite hours swaying past
with kings and cockatoos
ranging through the yard

rosellas swing from branches
or riffle husks for remnant seeds
and the bees, they gorge on wild lettuce
yellow flowers tumbling over paths

I hear them calling me to rise and dress
not miss this gift of time
alas no energy
I stumble, must return to bed

last night my lungs refused to work
the bellows blocked, would not inhale
took all my strength and force of mind
to grasp some inward air

enough for me to exhale again
cough, cough, cough and on!
an hour or more without control
head pressure pain, longing for release

today I must recover
listening, feeling reassured
the parrots with return
with silver-eyes and spinebills

tomorrow I shall be among them
and the graceful bee throng
long after lungs have ceased
to cause me such distress

the garden I have built will sustain
lives shorter than my own.

On Transience

Hold in your mind these few days
when the world outside transforms
it is autumn and death is life to come

we are never just observing
nor held separate from the world
we are a tree, an insect and the earth

we are the sky and tumbling water
today, this instant in time's continuum
I exist in soft animal form

tomorrow my star dust will devolve
break down to mineral parts
grow into its new measure

leaves twist in the breeze
colours change as they fall
a kaleidoscope of gold to ruby shades

this wonder, to watch my ancestors
and my children's children
what hope and fear to ponder.

Autumn April 25

It is the season of falling
streets fill with blazing leaves
they shed like tears
soon trees are standing bare

a time for remembering
the butchered lives of our young
green shoots of yesterday
we spent in foreign wars

one day to mark a nation's loss
dawn service held across the land
a lone bugle flaring
slow curling through the air

in the still of misted mornings
leaves mound like new-dug graves
this month of nature's sharing
grief that does not end.

Towards Winter

A time of quiet contemplation
half dreams in morning light
the air is honey-coloured
filtered through autumn layers

the shadowplay of bare branches
where our minds dissociate
from the needy hours ahead
the glare and blast of yesterday

outside a sweep of fallen leaves
cushions our steps, eager to be home
we are folding in upon ourselves
the body craves heat's comfort

we turn aside from the earth
as the garden prepares to sleep
we cook and plump, hibernate
in our own deep cave of reverie.

Waiting for the Wolf

Butterflies defy the gathering chill
these last shivers of light
dancing through autumn afternoons
and us settling down in our home
prepared for biting days ahead

I feel a sparseness in the air
as snails and other half-seen lives
disappear till spring
the burrowing frog for one
and those I do not wish to spy

a small grey mouse flicks past
scurries down the hall
it seeks the shelter of our rooms
knows my untidy dog
scatters treats on which to graze

fruit trees cast off their canopies
drop remnant apple cores
in morning mist and random showers
before the beast of winter
howls at our door again.

After the Party

They drop their flouncing petticoats
or gather them tightly
shy and softly fading
pink, white and red
the lights are dimmed
camellia season over

some stood out and shone
in perfect form and shading
the striped and boldly stippled
or ones of softer tones
suggesting sun-tinged clouds
of palest rose and peach

next year they will appear
surround me with their vibrance
depending on the climate
if not, these memories suffice
as bright and swirling skirts
limber on their branches,

Gentle as a Falling Cloud

As birds, rosellas red and blue
sidestep with care along wet branches
looking for the flowers of yesterday
snow falls, large luminous flakes
caught in a gust of air, they lift and flurry
settle on the new green shoots
drawn forth by last week's sunny days

a pure white crystal glare
heavy laden on each bough and leaf
as we inside curl into ourselves
soft animals wrapped in layers
our plans to tackle spreading weeds
prune for tomorrow's heat can wait
the threat of fires seems far away

for now we dream, feel safe
while elsewhere there are floods
flames ravage other island homes
our storms are yet to come
here we can make believe
the earth and climate are benign
light as the quilt of snow enclosing us today.

Nested

I wake to the extended arm of winter
observing life outside my home
this small patch of the natural world
sleeps through inclement seasons
but that is such a broad brushstroke

the winter apricot opens hands of light
as a wattlebird defends its larder
another curves through thin blue air
wind fidgets among perfumed jonquils
plump with buds ready to entice

a tangle of branches enclose the house
it is a nest, a living wall of protection
sheltering my rooms come hotter months
for now, there's time to doze and incubate
till I can chance my wings and fly.

A Promise in Winter

The prunus mume apricot
is strung with white blossom
and the shimmer of raindrops

wrapped in lichen collars
its spreading vase of limbs
is patchworked soft grey-green

each year I wait, impatient
for this herald of brighter months
to fill my winter window

wattlebirds swoop to its branches
raucously feast on nectar
scattering shards of white petals

as daffodils slowly open
our iced and dismal months
are coming to their end

soon the garden will transform
from dense and leafless thicket
to a perfumed greenery

insects, birds and lizards
will gather day and night, for now
this tree is a lantern in the dark.

Unwelcome

Days of ice and snow clouds
as a force comes beating
whistling through the trees

and when the light departs
when only sound remains
we hear the curtains shiver

wind prowls our frosty walls
it blows beneath the door
whines to be admitted
to our warmth and glow.

Aqua Vite

Snow falling through the trees
mist freezing on your skin
steaming on your breath

light as a breeze curls upward
to hail and rock-sharp ice
the glacial terrain

old and stagnant thick as mud
a racing roaring cataract
drenching tropic storms

floods and waves and wash
drowning out of depth
or floating buoyant as a raft

our tepid baths and drinks
boiling basting scalding
the comfort of hot tea

a burbling gurgling stream
shrinking in the sun
to drought-baked earth

hard parched and cracked
waiting praying yearning
for the sound of rain.

Cloudy With the Chance of Disaster

When the sky shines
its blue-glazed dome above our heads
and every leaf glows
in a pure green benediction
yet the day feels heavy as iron

I sense the force of change
an inclement wind is building
on the edge of our lives
where every breathing thing
down to the smallest life is under threat

We are prepared for towns to flood
know more sparks will kindle into fire
this is not an age of uncertainty
we see the coming storm
our turn this or next time.

Enduring

Scant majesty after fire
had left them desolate
they fell or leant diagonally

bare threads against the sky
rough bark still blacked
twenty years since they burnt

scar-worn they endure
shoot from the base and trunk
saplings strive up and out

with footholds grasped
the forest-scorched underground
must build to life again

small creatures range
in flame-split rock and crevice
find new shelters for their young

how soon we forget
and build within the bush
learn to live in danger's mouth.

I Listen to Their Passing

That bird I hear on waking
softly calling to the wind
tells me all breath is one

each life is shaped by change
and we are wanton with our power
discounting lives beyond our own

divorced from grass and loam
in homes we build on loss
tree hollows with their nests

forests fall and creatures die
that bird I heard before
is a memory, it may not call again.

A Pledge

We do not need an acre
one small pot will do
a little sun and water
with the time to care

in soil ripe for growing
the urge to live begins
with buds and leaves
one seed becomes a giant

as we unfold and flower
into our human grace
the promise we are making
is to nourish love of life.

Mellifluous

I speak for the bees
goddess pollinators of the earth
with gifts of wax and honey
they bring us fruit and nuts
our leafy green exuberance

grass, wheat and grains
seed with the wind
to fill their golden fields
but apples need insect love
and bees are in decline

their lives essential to our own
since bees and man began
now imagine food reduced
to imitation brands, lab-made
no ripening on the vine

this is the world we craft
divorced from native hives
choice is a splendid thing
if you are rich enough
to hold a strawberry in your hand.

No Second Coming, No Second Chance

When the birds stop singing
and the bees have given up their hives
when no moths dance around our lamps

we will look up to a shadeless sky
the harsh blue of shimmering heat
and talk of yesterdays we knew

as if a torpor bound us then
hoping for a climate change of heart
or some messiah to save us from regret

one to solve the planet's discontent
with a plan we'd all embrace
not asking us to sacrifice our easy life

the memory of comforts we demanded
slipping from our grasp, too late now
there's nothing we can buy to set it right.

Growth Overload

Last year evaded summer
of singlets, shorts and skin
thrumming insects overhead
and fledglings' constant squawks

we missed the bite of sunburn
and firefear-laden winds
each step on guard for snakes
watchful from the shadows

last year we dressed in gumboots
turned winter heaters on
witnessed rain squall battering
through waterboarding months.

Splooshed

Leaves droop, heavy with rain
lichen builds its layers up the stem
mosses flower on paths and stone
we slip and squelch like slugs

as heartbeats to our bodies
the pulse is same on same
sounds from falling water
flood the membrane of my days

the sun's a fugitive body
birds and reptiles, mammals
are sloshing in their homes
and I am drowning in my skin.

Still Life With Scrubbing Brush

We wake to sungleam
filtered through soaked leaves
rain's constancy abates

this land of drought and fire
plagued by water bombs
floods dominate the news

honeysuckle, brambles thrive
my paths unkempt, impassable
wrapped in creeping bands

the hours that I would spend
with fork and trowel outside
now inhouse gardening claims

mould blooms on chairs and walls
I clean and scrub, repeat
beside the constant hum of fans

weeks ebb and flow as tides
chilled and winter bare
days bleach to monochrome.

Seeking Shelter
for Rael

There is sunshine
coming after months of rain
with images of flood and mud
so many lives unmade

too soon the weather turned
the once in a life deluge
twice this year his home is wrecked
but the debt and loss remain

he can't face that shock again
just one family of the many
on the road in vans and tents
to find another life.

Lismore 2022

After their paths and garden beds
became creeks and dams
from skies of constant cloud

torrential rain swelled, swept
dirt and stone down council drains
their summer months awash

we saw river folk submerged
high set homes and streets drown
with rescue boat flotillas bailing fast

after this too-fast deluge
the stench of rotting mud, goods
thrown to the sweating verge

the waste of years and dreams
piled high as the failed levy
made empty pockets of their hearts.

In the Shadow of Pompeii

Unlivable tomorrow
our sleepy river towns
now their lives of comfort
end in flood on flood

a hundred years or more
to plan for these disasters
not to waste this finite time
while living soft and warm

our choice to sit and dream
now we burn and drown
as the climate roars in distress
a lava flow of destructive weather

like a volcano under pressure
rumbling through the years
we ignored her constant warnings
but knew she'd blow one day.

Crystals and Carbon

In the wild desert places
our ancient earth speaks to us
in grains of ochre-coloured sand
the scattering of charcoal sticks
hold words of fire and storm

from shallow seas and mountains
where opals formed and iron fell
aggregated into wealth
by tunnelling and blasts
we have become a geologic force

like ants who build their giant mounds
reshaping what had been
till it has passed from sight
we change the fertile land
into a tamed but lifeless space.

Ghostly

So many bright wings
in this exhibition
stuffed, pinned, poisoned, posed
our urge for possession
we studied without learning

the largest birdwing butterfly
glowing in its afterlife
as we go meekly filing past
noting skeletons and remnants
of talon, teeth and bone

I stop before our thylacine
a European tiger shares its case
this catalogue of extinctions in the wild
to see our crimes on display
I am haunted by their glassy eyes.

In the Age of Extinctions

Moon   a gentle name
for this humpback whale
each year she crossed the ocean
to her mating grounds
in warm Hawaiian shallows
the sea where she was born

obedient to her culture
Moon taught her calves
to breathe and breach
navigate the Pacific lanes
back to the ice of Canada
and feasts of two-inch krill

impelled to make her final journey
three thousand miles and more
she breaststroked, depleted
her back broken, tail paralysed
past speeding ships
that do not watch for whales.

Finding Our Backbone

Beyond the coastal limits
we find a sharp landscape
the scoliotic spine of country
where escarpments stretch north to south

fires lay bare these weathered bones
expose the ancient petroglyphs
lost stories of millennia
we took so long to comprehend

now a kindling flame of pride
has flickered into life
we embrace this sublime culture
once banned, degraded and defiled

our Eurocentric minds shipped from small fields
expand to understand
this land needs many stories
to frame its harsh design

we can't transplant rapacious laws
and hope the land survives
we learn through our mistakes
adapt, accept advice

the wonder is
a people we had striven to erase
are willing to forgive us
if we listen, side by side.

The Ancestors

They are here   always
walking across the land
like wind among the trees
they're passing through
to hunting, meeting grounds
with songs I do not hear

they are not my kin
I have no soul connection
other than what dollars buy
to clear and build
create new storylines
devoid of spirit life

we invaders do not know
the history of this place
who thrived and sheltered here
we erase a future for us all
through the creatures we expel
till only ghosts can sing.

On the Baaka

Dead-eyed they float
young bloated bodies
in their countless millions
reaching for one last breath

a bleaching canvas
exposed to sun and air
smothering the river surface
we paint extinction here

how many could they feed
or breed for unknown years
if their water had not died
been sold for other needs

and with the power of gods
we still give farmers more
than shrinking rivers hold
and take the fish's share.

Seeds of War

The past binds us to the earth
as we lift our faces up to life
oligarchs and despots
replace our dreams with theirs
blood sacrifice to the god of power

in Ukraine the war of '41
of Hitler's troops at Babi Yar
haunt the eyes of the aged
whose stories shaped the young
as the nightmare starts again

defiant to this new outrage
an old woman extends her fist
to the invading soldier in her street
she hands him sunflower seeds
so they can mark his grave.

With Wings to Fly

Where will the small bird go
sharp-eyed he ate the crumbs
from my balcony

every day we'd share
the morning sun together
tonight I gather papers, clothes

now my city lies in rubble
the park across the street
is a ghost of shattered branches

the bag I pack is heavy
but my coat and boots are strong
at first light I'll leave my home

join the ranks of the broken
who hope to reach the border
as guns are flaming round us

if my building falls tomorrow
where will that dear bird fly
or has it left before me
to a safety I can't know.

On Seeing

Look through your tears and loss
to light outside your room
in the sunshine glint on leaves
are boundless gifts of morning

as you curl inside your bed
see that small bird upon the stem
it is harvesting green aphids
there for your eyes, your ears

each day holds joys unknown
to touch and feel the pulse
of every breathing thing
and you are ready for its wonder.

Marvels

We come from the stars
exploding outward into us
this fiery dimension
settles down to layer on layer
as silt and dust and ash

from geologic slow to speed of light
as we patch our knowledge in
that fuzzy image, a foetus or new nebuli
life's work unseen and known
an egg, a sperm, then cells grow

soft shell and invertebrate
breathing, squirming, breeding on
of heart and blood and bone
the myriad complexity
that forms our fragile world.

From Where You Stand

Mists have gilded rock with lichen
in orange striations
blooming haloes of white
softly growing through the years
and I ponder how we live together

from earthworm to towering pine
the distortions of time in every lifeform
do we think ourselves well served
by the hours, years, millenia
allotted to our kind

this flux, malleable as being
in cloud-embracing trees
or urgent bee about its hive
and I the watcher, from my perspective
see them scurry or never move at all

while they observe me
as gnat or mountain tall
a flashing shadow or growling monolith
imperceptibly eroding into soil
from their point of view.

This Sacred Life

It is the passing moments
when my troubled heart rises
like a poppy bathed in sunlight
that I see our world is hallowed

it is the magpie calling to her mate
with a curling melody of love
and their swirl of notes together
here I touch the measure of my days

as a priestess of our random sphere
I have memories that are luminous
a sunset across ancient desert cliffs
the aurora above my childhood home

through the spinning of the seasons
from low cloud to summer blue
where changing moods of light
reveal the ephemeral as a holy state

the mind's repose is fragile
ever ready to retreat or waver
I look into my temple of fleeting images
here are votive candles to sustain me

I greet the morning as a healing mantle
as a tree awakening to growth
my heart cupped within its leaves
swells deep and boundless.

Shanghaied

There are spider boats
anchored to each plant
binding tree and shrub
from paling fence to wall

I step into their sticky sea
and return bedangled
wrapped in broken threads
on my hair and clothes

besieged by spider lines
everywhere I look
a lilliputian fishing fleet
casting nets of silk.

Those Indian Mynas

They jeer and swagger
jackhammer the air
with loud discordant notes

despised for murderous raids
where native chicks freefall
ejected from their nests

street wise and city smart
bullies of the 'hood
scavenging from bins

with flick-knife beaks
they strut like gangsters
menacing our path.

Exhaling

Relax
let the breeze
riffle through your hair
believe there is no rush
to be there or other place
feel the warmth of your blood
the rise and fall of breath
life's joy of being here
and nowhere else
but now.

Dancing with Van Gogh

He was an alchemist of light
his need to capture that pure colour
to match the buttercup and sunflower
as it sang within the meadows
of his summers in the south

he primed canvas with white lead
craved chrome yellow and its poisons
bold new colours, factory brewed
inhaled, licked the brush   obsessed
tones blended on his fingers

his one desire and purpose
a blindness drove him on
his layering of petals   soft butter
to harvest orange upon a lemon ground
building depth and deadly weight

such music in his head
of insect hum and random voices
a little madness   who has not?
when dreams were manifest
gold flowed from his dancing brush.

Free to Indulge

After our market trudge
we retreat downwind
of dumplings and paella
into the den of painted cakes

like children at a party
wanting sugar fancy dressed
eyes devour layered creations
pop at their extravagance

cerise orchids' op art shimmer
above plush green velvet couches
we gorge as five friends gather
like schoolgirls at a fete

a first meeting out of lockdown
we get high on their proximity
this surge of human vibrance
a cherry on the glaze of our excess.

The Little Princess

I do not know what she expected
from these strangers in her life
showering her with cuddles
then moulding her into their prize

fed by hand from high tables
food she never thought
could taste this good
at the top of the pile, head dog

learning she had power to attract
delighting in human attention
pats from everyone she met
bowing to her majesty.

Sandling

I tread drifts of cupped shells
open faces filled with brine
white, amber, purple hued
crunch beneath my soles

grey oysters interspersed
with swirls of florid weed
a playful gull swoops, teases
dogs barking at the waves

time lost among the dunes
my sand warmed heart
a winged leaf drawn to the beach
content and quite alone.

Unclocked

Our mornings salt encrusted
by the wave-jagged ocean
as parrots abandon trees
before the sun turns sharp

these slow-paced holidays
of breakfast indolence
celebrate our low tide days
no counting through the hours

soon the clock and its demands
will be a turnkey once again
for now our thoughts unwind
set free as coastal breeze.

Weekending

At dusk the river settles down to whispers
as a lilac sky shifts into mauve
its subtle permutations
against steel-grey-banded clouds

black darts, the homing lorikeets
flash vibrant green in horizontal sun
these miracles of sharp-edged flight
that cluster into silent dark

Sunday morning and sea fog quilts the town
homes slumber or stir bleary-eyed
no urgency of school and work
we hear them sigh, luxuriate.

The White-faced Heron

I step from the rush of waves
as a swallow dips and soars
scoops the updraft air

watching gulls dive and splash
how sorely earthbound do I feel
hobbled by my wingless state

but nor am I that timid wader
who pauses ever wary
haunting the edge of sand

it does not ask for more
than a frog among the reeds
this graceful slow-paced walker

we two are winter nomads
drawn to the ocean's edge
to the sun upon our backs.

Time and Tide

I sit, admire the breakers swell and boom
while a butcherbird pours liquid notes
romances the passage of its day

I'm sheltered in a nook of rocks
green serpentine, jagged, worn
scrunched by heat and aged

here olivine sparkles in the sun
as a casuarina sighs above my head
elbows leaning on the hip of sand

the beach is etched by foot and paw
rituals of the day we share
this hour, this place and now

how quickly our lives are swept along
in breaths that rise and fall
an ocean tumbling to its shore.

Finding My Place

The mountains at distance
are blue as the morning ocean
within their shield of dense forest
how many lives do they protect

in low sun, birds gather on the sand
finding heat for the day ahead
a time of communal simplicity
as a sea mist envelops the horizon

beneath a cloudless winter sky
I encounter the changing vista
by afternoon the water turns
it is the colour of antique pewter

the interweaving of time's layers
the cycles of rise and fall
of which I am so brief a part
nor wishing to be greater.

Acknowledgements

I wish to thank my editor Brendan Doyle for his careful reading and advice. Gratitude is also due to my publishers, Ginninderra Press, in their dedication to the independent voice.

My husband deserves more than loving thanks – he listened with forbearance as I intoned many versions of these poems on their way to completion.

'With Wings to Fly' previously appeared in The Crow.

'In the Age of Extinctions' appeared in The Amphibian.

I live on the unceded lands of the Yaluk-ut Weelam of the Boon Wurrung and the Darug and Gundungurra people. I pay my respects to the traditional owners and to elders past and present.

www.ingramcontent.com/pod-product-compliance
Lightning Source LLC
Chambersburg PA
CBHW072132070526
44585CB00016B/1640

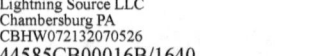